Ocean Animals
MANATEES

By Walter LaPlante

Please visit our website, www.garethstevens.com. For a free color catalog of all our high-quality books, call toll free 1-800-542-2595 or fax 1-877-542-2596.

Library of Congress Cataloging-in-Publication Data

Names: LaPlante, Walter, author.
Title: Manatees / Walter LaPlante.
Description: New York : Gareth Stevens Publishing, [2020] | Series: Ocean animals
Identifiers: LCCN 2019010483| ISBN 9781538244579 (paperback) | ISBN 9781538244593 (library bound) | ISBN 9781538244586 (6 pack)
Subjects: LCSH: Manatees--Juvenile literature.
Classification: LCC QL737.S63 L36 2020 | DDC 599.55--dc23
LC record available at https://lccn.loc.gov/2019010483

First Edition

Published in 2020 by
Gareth Stevens Publishing
111 East 14th Street, Suite 349
New York, NY 10003

Copyright © 2020 Gareth Stevens Publishing

Designer: Katelyn E. Reynolds
Editor: Kristen Rajczak Nelson

Photo credits: Cover, pp. 1, 5 Jeff Stamer/Shutterstock.com; pp. 7, 17 gary powell/Shutterstock.com; pp. 9, 24 (tail) Bildagentur Zoonar GmbH/Shutterstock.com; p. 11 Shirley Jeanne Robinson/Shutterstock.com; pp. 13, 24 (seagrasses) feel4nature/Shutterstock.com; p. 15 Enrique Aguirre/Shutterstock.com; pp. 19, 24 (calves) Greg Amptman/Shutterstock.com; p. 21 Liquid Productions, LLC/Shutterstock.com; p. 23 somdul/Shutterstock.com.

All rights reserved. No part of this book may be reproduced in any form without permission in writing from the publisher, except by a reviewer.

Printed in the United States of America

CPSIA compliance information: Batch #CW20GS: For further information contact Gareth Stevens, New York, New York at 1-800-542-2595.

Contents

Underwater Living 4

Time to Eat! 12

Manatee Life 16

See One! 22

Words to Know 24

Index 24

Manatees live in the ocean!

They like warm water.

7

Flat tails help them swim.

They come up for air!

They eat seagrasses.

13

They are called
sea cows.

They swim alone or in small groups.

Babies are calves.

They are
born underwater!

21

You may see one
at the zoo!

Words to Know

calves   seagrasses   tail

Index

babies 18   water 6
food 12   zoo 22